Thanksgiving

Why We Celebrate It the Way We Do

by Martin Hintz and Kate Hintz

CAPSTONE PRESS

MANKATO

C A P S T O N E   P R E S S

818 North Willow Street • Mankato, MN 56001

Printed in the United States of America.

Library of Cataloging-in-Publication Data
Hintz, Martin
    Thanksgiving : why we celebrate it the way we do / by
    Martin and Kate Hintz.
    48 p. cm. ill (some col.)
    Includes bibliographical references and index.
    Summary: Describes the origins of Thanksgiving and how we celebrate the
    holiday.
    ISBN 1-56065-328-0
    1. Thanksgiving Day--Juvenile literature. [1. Thanksgiving Day.]
    I. Hintz, Kate. II. Title.
    GT4975.H57   1996
    394.2'649--dc20   95-25928
                      J NF 394.2649   CIP
                      HINTZ   AC

Photo credits:
FPG International/Ron Chapple: p. 4; Dick Luria: pp. 32-33
Archive Photos: pp. 6, 7, 13, 14, 18, 25, 27, 40.
Paula Borchardt: p. 8
Visuals Unlimited/E.Webber: p. 17; Arthur Gurmankin: p. 21; Joe McDonald:
p. 22; M. Long: pp. 31, 43; Leonard Lee Rue III: p. 38; Len Rue Jr.: cover.
Peter Ford: pp. 29, 36.

Cornbread recipes by Sara Steever and Tami Deedrick.

Table of Contents

Words in **boldface** type in the text are defined
in the Glossary in the back of this book.

Chapter 1
Giving Thanks

Thanksgiving is a time to give thanks. It is a time to remember the blessings of the past year.

Thanksgiving Day is a national holiday in the United States. It celebrates the Pilgrims coming to North America. It honors the Pilgrims' hard work and faith. They were thankful for their new land. They were thankful for their freedom.

Thanksgiving is a time to give thanks for having enough to eat.

The first Thanksgiving was celebrated by the Pilgrims and the Wampanoags.

Celebrating the Harvest

But Thanksgiving is not just an American idea. It is celebrated throughout the world. It celebrates a good harvest. Harvesting means bringing in crops. People all over the world work hard for months to have a good harvest.

Different foods are harvested at different times of the year. That means people celebrate their harvests at different times.

Some people name their celebrations. These are called harvest festivals. The reason for a harvest festival is always the same. It is a time to give thanks for food.

People all over the world celebrate the harvest.

Chapter 2

Thanksgiving History

People have been giving thanks for centuries. Ancient people thanked their gods for taking care of them. Many of their ceremonies celebrated the harvest of food. Their ways of celebrating have affected our own Thanksgiving celebration.

The Egyptians

The ancient Egyptians depended on the Nile River. The Nile watered their crops. At harvest time, the Egyptians thanked the gods of the

Native Americans celebrate every time they have a harvest. One of their thanksgivings is the corn festival.

Nile. They sacrificed fruit, grain, and animals to the gods.

The Greeks

Greek people believed that different gods controlled the rain, sun, and wind. When there was a good harvest, the Greeks celebrated with a festival. They thanked the gods that helped grow the food.

The Romans

Long ago, the Roman people honored the goddess of grain. Her name was Ceres. In October, they thanked her with parades, speeches, music, and dancing. People ate a lot of food. The Romans believed that Ceres helped grow the wheat, grapes, olives, and other food. The word cereal comes from Ceres.

The Mayans

The Mayans have lived in Mexico and Central America for hundreds of years. They eat turkey at their harvest festival. Corn is an important part of the celebration, too.

Early England

In early England, farmers believed a spirit lived in their crops. They thought the spirit made the plants healthy.

The English farmers celebrated a good harvest. Flowers decorated the last wagon of grain brought in from the fields. People sang, danced, and thanked the spirit in the plants.

The Chinese

The Chinese people believed that the moon plowed the heavens. They had a ceremony called Chung Ch'ui. It honored the moon. People made moon cakes from freshly harvested grain.

Bulgaria

In Bulgaria, the last stalk of corn harvested from the field was special. The farmers dressed it in women's clothes. It was called the corn queen.

The Bulgarian farmers carried the corn queen through the village. They took it to a pond or stream and drowned it. The Bulgarians thought this would bring enough rain for the next year's crops.

Native Americans

Throughout their history, Native Americans have celebrated every time they harvested something. They have many celebrations during the year.

In the green corn ceremony, they thank the Great Spirit. At the corn festival, they ask for blessings.

Today, most Native Americans do not take part in the American Thanksgiving. This holiday celebrates European people coming to America. Native Americans believe the European **settlers** stole their land.

Squanto was an interpreter between the Pilgrims and the Native Americans.

Chapter 3

The Pilgrims and Thanksgiving

Hundreds of years ago, if people complained about the Church of England, they were charged with treason. Treason is the crime of being unfaithful to your country.

One group of people did not like the Church of England. They were upset that religious holidays became parties instead of prayer

The Pilgrims met Samoset and Massasoit, who was the chief of the Wampanoag nation.

services. They wondered why no one seemed to care about poor and hungry people.

This group left the Church of England in the early 1600s. They wanted to worship God in their own way. They were called **Separatists**.

They wore plain clothes and worked hard. They helped the poor. They were accused of treason. Many lost their jobs. Some were put in prison.

They decided to leave England. They wanted a place where they could worship in peace. They called their trip a pilgrimage. A pilgrimage is a long journey to a holy place. Later, these people were known as **Pilgrims**.

The Pilgrims

The Pilgrims had heard of a land across the Atlantic Ocean. They called it the New World. It was a land of riches. No one would bother them there.

The Pilgrims found people to give them money for their trip. In return, the Pilgrims agreed to work for the people. They promised to send back furs and other valuables. They would work for seven years.

The people with money talked other people into going on the trip. These people were not Pilgrims. They agreed to work for seven years, too.

They all left from Plymouth, England on September 16, 1620. Their ship was called the **Mayflower**.

The Pilgrims sailed aboard the Mayflower.

They landed in what is now Massachusetts on December 26. They called their new town Plymouth, after the town they had left behind.

Samoset and Squanto

In the spring, a Native American man came to Plymouth. His name was Samoset. He had learned English from fishermen who had sailed to his land.

Samoset had the Pilgrims meet Massasoit who was chief of the Wampanoag nation. He also had them meet his friend Squanto.

Squanto had been kidnapped by English explorers in 1614. They took him to Spain. He worked as an **interpreter**.

Squanto returned to his native land in 1618. All of his people had died while he was away. He moved into Massasoit's village.

The Pilgrims called their new town Plymouth.

Helping the Pilgrims

Squanto became friends with the Pilgrims. He showed them how to fish in the rivers. He showed them how to plant corn. He helped them build houses. Their crops stood tall and healthy.

Everyone was thankful for surviving the winter. The Pilgrims decided to hold a harvest feast. They wanted to thank God for their good crops.

The exact date of this gathering is not known. It probably took place after the autumn harvest of 1621.

The Feast

The Pilgrims invited Massasoit and his people to the feast. The Wampanoags brought five deer for the huge dinner. The Pilgrim men shot ducks, geese, and turkeys. The women made cakes, puddings, and roasted corn.

Wild turkeys are found only in North America. They were the main course.

**The homes of Plymouth colony were built of wood.
A wooden fence protected the town.**

Cranberries grew wild. They were part of the feast.

The eating and parties went on for three days. Everyone played games. The Pilgrims marched. They fired their muskets. The Native Americans showed their skill with bows and arrows.

Chapter 4

A Tradition Grows

Many more **colonies** were established. The colonists had festivals and feasts. They gave thanks through the year.

The colonists were thankful for different reasons. Some gave thanks for weddings and births. Some were thankful for the arrival of friends from across the ocean. Others were thankful for rain and good weather.

Wild turkeys are found only in North America.

Thanks for Victory

The king of England wanted to continue to control the colonies. The colonists wanted to be free. They fought a war against each other. It was called the **Revolutionary War**. It started in 1775.

During the war, the colonists gave thanks when they won a battle. They celebrated with prayers and a good meal.

The war ended in 1783. The colonies had won their independence. The **Continental Congress** proclaimed a day of thanks. But there was no official Thanksgiving holiday.

Washington Honors the Constitution

After the war, the colonies joined together. They became the United States of America. George Washington was elected the first president.

Washington wanted to honor the new **Constitution** of the United States. He set aside November 26, 1789, as an official day of thanks.

Sarah Josepha Hale worked to make Thanksgiving a national holiday.

Sarah Josepha Hale's Idea

In the mid-1800s, Sarah Josepha Hale edited a famous magazine called *Godey's Lady's Book*. She wrote articles suggesting a national Thanksgiving day. Many of her readers started to celebrate a special day of thanks.

This idea went west with the **pioneers**. By the 1850s, most states celebrated an official Thanksgiving. Each state governor chose the day. The day was different from state to state.

Families loved getting together for those early Thanksgivings. They got ready weeks before the celebration. Women made pies and cakes. Men hunted and dug vegetables. Children helped in the kitchen or around the farm.

People brought baskets of food to their minister and schoolteacher. Gifts were considered part of their wages. The poor received gifts from wealthy neighbors.

Lincoln Proclaims a Legal Holiday

States from the North and South fought each other in the Civil War (1861-1865). Abraham Lincoln was president at the time. He announced national days of thanks after Northern victories.

President Lincoln proclaimed the last Thursday of November a national Thanksgiving holiday.

Lincoln wanted to show people they had much to be thankful for. He thought they should be thankful even during a war.

After the North won the war, Lincoln set aside the last Thursday of November as the official Thanksgiving Day.

Congress made Thanksgiving Day official in 1941.

Canada Celebrates Thanksgiving

The Thanksgiving holiday in Canada has many different beginnings.

The Canadian Thanksgiving is held on the second Monday of October.

One of the first to celebrate a Canadian Thanksgiving was John Frobisher. He was an English explorer. He came to Canada in 1578. He gave thanks when he landed safely.

Other Thanksgiving days were marked over the years. They usually marked the end of a war or a victory in battle.

The first official Canadian Thanksgiving Day was held in November 1879. Many people thought it was too close to Christmas. There were several date changes. Since 1957, Canada has celebrated Thanksgiving on the second Monday of October.

Chapter 5

How We Celebrate

In North America, Thanksgiving is filled with food and fun. At the center of the celebration is the family.

Families At Home

Families get together at home on Thanksgiving Day. They come to share the holiday.

Food is a Thanksgiving tradition. Almost everyone has a turkey with mashed potatoes

Turkey is the traditional main course of Thanksgiving.

and gravy. They have stuffing and cranberry sauce. They have corn and yams. Pumpkin pie with whipped cream is the usual dessert.

Many families gather to watch the traditional Thanksgiving Day football games. It is a popular afternoon pastime.

Celebrating Outside the Home

Some cities have parades on Thanksgiving Day. People meet along the streets to watch. Floats and marching bands pass by. Giant balloons and clowns dance. Horses and motorcycles ride together. Some big cities show their parades on television.

Some families go to church for a Thanksgiving service. They pray like the Pilgrims did. They give thanks for the blessings of the past year.

Some families share with others. They serve food at homeless shelters. Others invite people who are alone to dinner.

Thanksgiving Decorations

Many people decorate their homes with fall colors for Thanksgiving. They use orange, brown, and yellow. Some people decorate with pumpkins and corn. They put stalks of corn by the door. Turkeys and Pilgrims are other common decorations.

A cornucopia is another decoration. It is a basket shaped like a horn. People fill it with fruits and vegetables. It is an ancient symbol of harvest. Sometimes it is called the horn of plenty.

Hurricane Thanksgiving

The U.S. Virgin Islands are in the Caribbean Sea. They are owned by the United States. People in the Virgin Islands celebrate a Hurricane Thanksgiving. They give thanks for living through the hurricane season.

Chapter 6

Things to Do for Thanksgiving

Y ou can celebrate Thanksgiving in many ways. Here are some ideas.

Make Cornbread

For many people, cornbread is part of the Thanksgiving meal. Here are two ways to make cornbread.

Mix one box of cornbread mix according to the package directions. Set it aside. Cook one-

Many families spend time together at Thanksgiving.

The turkey has become an important symbol of Thanksgiving.

half cup of chopped onion and one-half cup of chopped green pepper in three tablespoons of butter over medium heat for a short time. The onions and pepper will become soft and lightly browned.

38

Add the cooked vegetables to the cornbread mixture. Then, add one can of chopped green chilies and half a can of creamed corn. Mix well.

Pour the mixture into a greased 9x9-inch baking pan. Place the cornbread in an oven preheated to 375 degrees. Bake for 25 to 30 minutes. The top should be golden brown.

Stick a wooden toothpick in the center. If it is still clean when you pull it out, the cornbread is ready to eat. When the cornbread is still warm, pour melted butter over it.

Some people like sweet cornbread. Here is an easy recipe. In a large bowl, mix together the following ingredients: one box of cornbread mix, one cup of melted butter, one can of creamed corn, one can of drained whole kernel corn, eight ounces of sour cream, and two beaten eggs. Mix well and pour into a 9x13-inch pan. Bake at 350 degrees for one hour.

Make a Paper Turkey

Benjamin Franklin was a famous American. He wanted the turkey to be the national bird for the new United States. Other people wanted the bald eagle for the national symbol.

Benjamin Franklin wanted the turkey to be the national bird.

Even though the bald eagle was chosen, Franklin thought the turkey was a better choice. The turkey was native to North America. Eagles can be found in other countries.

You can draw your own turkey. Put your hand on a piece of paper with your fingers apart. Trace around your fingers. This is the outline for the turkey's body. Where you have drawn around your fingers are the feathers. The outline of your thumb is the head and neck. Now use crayons to color your bird.

Another turkey can be made from a paper plate. Glue strips of colored construction paper around the top of the plate. These are the feathers. Glue on macaroni for the eyes and beak.

Be creative. You can make your hand turkey or paper plate turkey as complicated as you like. Use real feathers. Add beads, glitter, or foil. Use your imagination to make the best turkey you can.

Feed the Hungry

Sharing is a big part of Thanksgiving. You can collect food for a homeless shelter or food pantry. You can help serve dinner. You can invite people who live alone over to visit. This will help make sure everyone has a family on Thanksgiving.

You can collect money for famine relief. Many countries in the world do not have enough food. Give your money to a United Nations group or a similar charity group.

Give Thanks

Make a list of everything you are thankful for. You can include your family, your pets, your jobs, your home, and your friends.

Put down anything you can think of. Read the list before you eat your Thanksgiving meal.

Write a letter to someone you appreciate. Thank them for being themselves. The letter can go to your mom or dad. It can go to your brother or sister, or your grandparents. You can

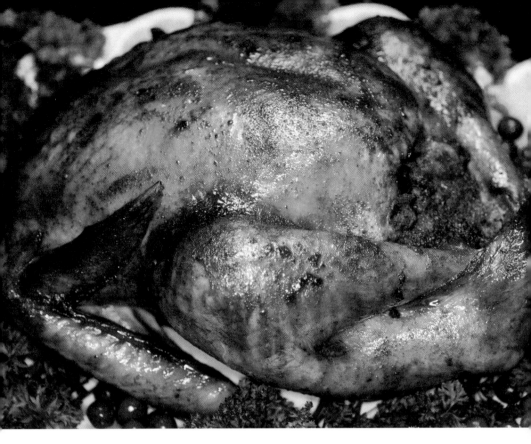

Sharing what you have with others who are less fortunate is a great way to celebrate Thanksgiving.

write to a special teacher or friend. Write more than one letter. People like to be remembered.

Make your own Thanksgiving traditions. Making the holiday your own is the best part of Thanksgiving.

Glossary

colonies—groups of people who settle in distant lands but remain subject to their native country

Congress—the group of elected people who make laws for the United States

Constitution—the document that is the basic law of the United States

Continental Congress—the group of people who made laws for the colonies

famine—serious shortage of food resulting in widespread hunger and death

interpreter—a person who orally translates a conversation from one language to another

Pilgrims—the English Separatists who settled in North America

pioneers—the first people to settle a region

Revolutionary War—the war fought by the colonies to become independant of England

Separatists—English religious protestors who left the Church of England

settlers—people who make their home in a new country

To Learn More

Applebaum, Diana Karter. *Thanksgiving: An American Holiday, An American History.* New York: Facts on File, 1985.

Barkin, Carole, and Elizabeth James. *Happy Thanksgiving!* New York: Lothrop, Lee & Shepard Books, 1987.

Barth, Edna. *Turkeys, Pilgrims and Indian Corn.* New York: The Seabury Press, 1975.

Clesi, Teresa. *Squanto and the First Thanksgiving.* Austin, Texas: Raintree Steck-Vaughn, 1992.

Linton, Ralph and Adelin Linton. *We Gather Together: The Story of Thanksgiving.* Detroit: Omnigraphics, 1990.

McGovern, Ann. *The Pilgrims' First Thanksgiving.* New York: Scholastic, 1973.

Penner, Lucille Recht. *The Thanksgiving Book.* New York: Hastings House, 1985.

Useful Addresses

Canadian Turkey Marketing Agency
44 Peel Centre Drive #403
Brompton, ON L6T 4B5
Canada

General Society of Mayflower Descendants
Winslow Street
Plymouth, MA 02360

National Turkey Federation
11319 Sunset Hills Road
Reston, VA 22090

National Wild Turkey Federation
Box 530, Wild Turkey Building
Edgefield, VA 24824

Native Council of Canada
384 Bank Street
Ottawa, ON K2P 1Y1
Canada

Pilgrim Society
Pilgrim Hall Museum
75 Court Street
Plymouth, MA 02360

Plimoth Plantation
Box 1620
Plymouth, MA 02362

Survival of American Indians Association
7803-A Samurai Drive SE
Olympic, WA 98500

Index